FREE TO BE

Free to Be

Also by Dale Turner and available from High Tide Press:

Different Seasons: Twelve Months of Wisdom & Inspiration
Grateful Living
Another Way: Open-Minded Faithfulness

FREE TO BE

Teaching Stories by:
Dr. Dale Turner

Illustrations by:
Ross Smart

High Tide Press   2003

Published by High Tide Press Inc.
3650 West 183rd Street, Homewood, Illinois 60430

Turner, Dr. Dale E. Free to Be / by Dale Turner

ISBN 1-892696-28-2

Printed in China

Edited by Angel Summer & Timothy Williams
Book design by Nann Alleman of Bugeyedezine

For ordering information call 888.231.7229

Printed on acid free paper

To my grandchildren:

Aaron, Robin, Matthew, Heather,
Brittany, Evan, Carl, Marshall and Russell

Acknowledgements

Any success of my ministry is because I have always been half of a team. During my lifetime as a pastor, my wife of over 50 years, Leone, has been my teammate. A gifted singer and musician, she helped bring life to each church. She has directed literally hundreds of children and adults in choirs and concerts. We have been fortunate to have had a full, supportive and deeply loving marriage. None of my church work, community activities and weekly articles for the religion section of The Seattle Times, are mine alone; they are also Leone's. I cherish our life and work together.

It is common to thank one's publisher. I would like to do more than simply acknowledge Tim Williams. He has been a driving force in the publishing of all of my books. He has brought a wealth of skills to this work. Sometimes it seems he can single handedly publish books as if by magic. He has worked tirelessly to make all these books become a reality. He is a good man and has become a good friend.

Also, I would be amiss if I did not mention Ross Smart and Angel Summer. Ross is the young man whose wacky sense of humor and gifts as an artist led to the wonderful, whimsical illustrations that punctuate this book. Angel edited the sermonettes, turning a transcript of the spoken word into lucid, easy to read prose.

There are also three young critics who helped shape this book. Each primary school aged student read more than a hundred stories, providing concise and helpful feedback on every portion. Each brought his or her own special talents and viewpoint to this work. It is a pleasure and an honor to thank Matthew Peters, Katie Hovanes, and Kellen Rosburg. Their enthusiasm, insights and persistent hard work have been an inspiration.

Lastly, I thank Ruth Williamson-Kirkland who resurrected these children's sermons from dusty files, filled in missing sections, laughed with me over stories about the happenings on the Sundays I delivered them and is generally "my girl Friday" who works on Thursdays (and sometimes on Mondays, Tuesdays and Wednesdays as well).

"Choices are a part of the whole of life.
We live in an unfinished world.
We are continuously shaping our own
lives, and the world in which we live,
by the choices we make."

Dr. Dale Turner

Preface

When I graduated from West Virginia Wesleyan College in 1940, I held in one hand a scholarship from Columbia University for graduate studies to become a football coach, and, in the other hand, a second scholarship for Divinity School at Yale University to become a minister. It was a "close call" for me to make, but I decided upon the road leading to the ministry and I have not looked back since. For over 40 years I was the minister for several Congregational Churches, my final 25 years at the University Congregational Church in Seattle, Washington.

Yet, the ministry often provided a wonderful opportunity for the part of me who loved coaching. The beginning of every service was a time for the young people. I invited them to come forward and sit with me on the stairs as I shared a story. Having worked my way through college and seminary as a magician, I enjoyed putting some special magic in each story.

The Seattle Zoo was most generous in lending various animals from giant tortoises that the children could ride, to an antelope, little monkeys and others. Members of the congregation also lent their own animals, equipment or skills. Story time was fun time that even the oldsters looked forward to. I know that I did!

But the stories were always meant to do more than just amuse and entertain. They were meant to teach a life lesson, to encourage, helping bring out the specialness of each child. This was the coaching.

The stories were at times my own creation; others were taken from real life, or adapted from old fables. Thirty of the stories have been recreated in this collection and wonderfully illustrated. Do not expect dusty old religious stories and words of heavy-handed preaching. Expect instead, joyful, instructive, fun reading. Imagine you have invited a magician into your home to entertain you. But this magician plans that once he has your mouth open in amazement, he will have some wisdom for you to swallow.

The title of this book Free to Be was chosen because I have a profound belief that we are all born with different combinations of innate potentialities. What each of us ultimately becomes is a reflection of our choices. Children can be trained and nurtured to create, to trust, to love and to be of service. Or they can make other choices that are harmful to themselves and society. Ultimately each child makes his or her own free to be choices and the role of the caring/loving parent, grandparent, relative or teacher is to help guide these choices.

Towards this end, each of the teaching stories is followed by a chat box filled with questions that can be used to promote discussion. Children will grow not only by hearing the stories but also through constructive dialogue.

Now, read as a parent, grandparent, a family or as a beloved friend. There is a coach at the sidelines rooting for you to use the magic in these teaching stories as a vehicle to spend quality time with your children. They are intended to encourage wisdom, compassion, generosity and joy.

Dale Turner

List of Stories

The Clouds That Wouldn't Cry

There once was a valley that was very sad. No rain had fallen upon it for many weeks. The grass was brown, the flowers sat with drooping heads, the trees were unhappy, the birds wouldn't sing, and the dust was very restless.

The wind passed over the valley and saw that everything was dry and lifeless. "Oh, this is sad, very sad," she thought. "I must find my cloud friends and ask for their help." So, the wind swooshed off to find some clouds.

The first cloud she found was a small pink cloud. She told her the sad story about the valley. "Please, come and cry over the valley so that all will be fresh again." "Oh, no thanks," replied the pink cloud.

"I can't. My dress will get all wet and fade. I'd like to help, but you'll have no trouble finding someone else to do it."

The wind hurried on and found a big, heavy, black cloud. "Will you help?" asked the wind. "Please, come and cry over the valley so that all will be fresh again." "I'd rather not right now," said the black cloud. "I think it's a good idea, but I'd rather wait and see what the others do." The wind did not want to argue, so she quickly moved on.

Soon the wind came to a little gray cloud. "Please, come and cry over the valley so that all will be fresh again," said the wind. "Oh, what could I do?" asked the cloud. "I'm so small; I'd only be a drop in a bucket. I can't make a difference. I'm thankful you've given me so many free rides through the sky, but you should see my schedule. I'm very busy." The wind was disappointed, but hurried on to try to find help for the valley.

She very quickly found several clouds playing together. "Hi everyone!" said the wind. "If you will help, you could really do some good. Please, come and cry over the valley so that all will be fresh again." The reply was the same. "We think it's a good idea, and we'd really like to help, but we're busy playing ball. After that, we're going to play hide and seek. It would be better if you could find someone else to do it."

Discouraged, but still determined, the wind moved on until she came to a dainty cloud flitting through the sky. The wind told the same story about the need for rain. "Please, come and cry over the valley so that all will be fresh again." "Oh, dear me, that is dreadful, simply dreadful," replied the dainty cloud. "Someone should do something. The valley just isn't what it used to be. Oh, dear me, dear me..." And the dainty cloud, wringing her hands, hurried on and found a place where she could float and worry.

By now, the wind was not only upset, but also quite angry. "This is awful!" she thundered. "These clouds were born to help. They

should bring fresh showers to the thirsty flowers, but they refuse to do anything! I am going to blow them all together so that they will bump their heads!" The powerful wind huffed and puffed as hard as she could. The dust billowed, leaves began flying through the air and the clouds all began to run into one another. They bumped their heads and began to cry. Suddenly, the rain came pouring down over the sad valley.

Soon the little blades of grass began to straighten up. They looked sharp in their new green jackets. The flowers began to smile and lift their colorful heads toward the sun. The trees moved their arms in delight and clapped their hands. The dust settled down and the birds began to sing. It was a beautiful sight to behold! The valley was fresh and green and peaceful once again. "Ah...," said the clouds. "Let us never be in such a hurry, or too busy, to help our friends in need."

CHAT BOX

1. How could the clouds have prevented getting their heads bumped together?

2. One of the clouds seemed to be quite worried about the valley, but all she did was run off by herself and worry some more. Did all her worrying help?

3. The group of clouds that was playing hide-and-seek seemed to think that their game was more important than the dry valley. Did they have to give up their fun in order to help? Explain.

4. Why were the clouds so pleased after they rained on the valley?

The Happiest Man in the Kingdom

Many years ago, there was a king who had everything, or at least it seemed that way. He had power, fame, and riches. There was one thing he did not have, however. The king was not happy. Most of the time, the king sat around feeling glum and gloomy, moody and melancholy. "Surely," he thought, "there must be someone in my kingdom who is joyful. If I could find that person and wear his shoes for one week, perhaps I would be able to capture some of his happiness."

So the king sent his servants out to find the happiest man in the kingdom. They traveled all over the land in search of the person who owned the shoes that would make the king happy. One day as the servants walked next to a large hedge, they heard a man whistling and humming. He continued to whistle and hum and soon broke out into joyous song. The king's attendants knew that this person was most definitely the happiest man around. They leapt over the hedge and noticed that the man was down on his hands and knees weeding his flower garden. They reached out and grabbed the man's ankles. He did not seem frightened and continued to try to pull up weeds.

The attendants noticed that the man had no shoes, which clearly meant that he had very little wealth. "How can you be so happy when you don't even have enough money for shoes?" one of the servants asked. "I hadn't thought about it," replied the man, while trying to pull up another stubborn weed. "I suppose I simply enjoy doing what I do, and I keep busy doing it."

The king's attendants released the man and returned to the castle with no shoes to offer the king. Although the king was not pleased that he could not "borrow" someone else's happiness, he realized that the happy man had taught him an important lesson. Oftentimes, the happiest moments that we experience are when we "lose" ourselves in productive work, a creative task, or helping others. Sometimes it is when we are writing a letter, planting a tree, cooking a meal, or even sweeping the floor. The king was so "busy" sitting around being unhappy that he forgot about the pleasures of being helpful or doing a simple job.

CHAT BOX

1. True happiness can be found in some of the little things that need to be done in the world around us. Is there a fun "job" that you do that others might describe as a boring chore?

2. Do you sing, hum or whistle when you are happy?

3. The king spent a lot of time trying to find out how he could attain someone else's happiness. How could he have better spent his days?

Bargain Lemonade

One hot summer day, a businesswoman drove home from work and spotted a young boy selling lemonade in his front yard. There was a big sign that read, "BARGAIN LEMONADE – 50 cents a glass!" "Well," she thought, "It's good to see a young businessperson being so industrious. I'll help him out." After drinking one glass, she decided to buy another. The price was too good to resist. She paid the boy one dollar and commended him for starting out early in life to learn how to run a business.

As the woman drove farther down the street, she saw another sign that read "LEMONADE – 75 cents per glass!" "Well," she thought,

"I've had all I want, but if I help one out, I should help the other one out too."

She got out of her car and bought a glass of lemonade from the boy. "May I ask why you are selling your lemonade for 75 cents?" she asked. "The boy down the street is selling his for only 50 cents. You may not get as many customers if you don't meet the price of your competitors."

"Oh," replied the child, "that's easy to explain. You see, earlier today, when I was riding my bike past his house, he was playing fetch with his dog. He had a big container of lemonade sitting on his porch steps. As I was ready to ride off, I heard him shouting, 'No, Blackie, no!' When I looked, he was trying to get his dog to stop drinking

from the lemonade container. Next thing I knew, he was changing the price on his sign. And that's the whole story, Ma'am. I figured that since I spent more time on quality control, I had a more valuable product."

With eyes opened wide and a chagrinned look on her face, the shrewd businesswoman got into her car and drove off. She felt a bit queasy while imagining a hot, thirsty, hairy, drooling dog slurping out of the same batch of lemonade she drank from. The woman wasn't sure if it was the added dog germs making her feel sick, or if it was simply the thought of it all.

On her way home, she realized that although she was a successful businesswoman, she had forgotten a very important fact – you normally get what you pay for! The second boy knew that since his lemonade was of higher quality than the other boy's, he felt confident in charging a little more money.

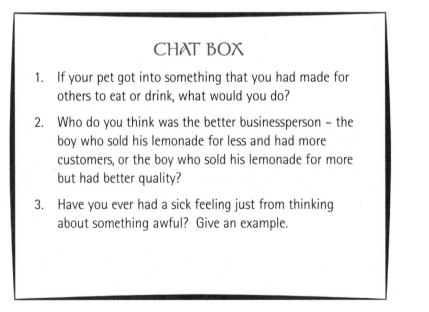

CHAT BOX

1. If your pet got into something that you had made for others to eat or drink, what would you do?

2. Who do you think was the better businessperson – the boy who sold his lemonade for less and had more customers, or the boy who sold his lemonade for more but had better quality?

3. Have you ever had a sick feeling just from thinking about something awful? Give an example.

NO, ME!

MINE!

NO, I DO!

The Nicest Hands

Kayla, Brady, and Emma were walking home from school together. They were just about to part ways when Emma said, "I don't know why I should mention this, but I just looked at my hands. They are so clean and nicely shaped. I think I have the nicest looking hands of all." Kayla looked at Emma's hands and said, "Well, they are pretty, but mine aren't so bad either." Brady laughed "Well, girls..." he said, "...my hands are clean and nice-looking too – as nice as either of yours!"

The friends stood at the corner and began to argue about who had the nicest hands. Finally, Brady said, "We're never going to solve our argument this way. Why don't we meet again tomorrow and stop the first person who goes by and ask who he or she thinks has the nicest hands? Whatever that person says will be final." They all agreed and hurried home.

Each child wanted to have the best hands for the next day's contest. Kayla heard that soaking them in buttermilk would make them appear fresh and gleaming. So, Kayla used up the last of the buttermilk and soaked her hands for almost an hour.

Emma heard that soaking in strawberry juice would make hands glowing and flawless. Emma went out to pick fresh strawberries and squeezed the juice out of them with a fork. She soaked her hands in the juice while she watched her favorite TV program.

Brady, too, did not want to be outdone. He wanted to prove to his friends that his hands could be as clean and handsome as ever. He had heard that if he bathed his hands in the morning dew from the grass and the leaves, that they would appear spotless. He pressed many leaves together and scooped dew off the grass. He collected a whole glass of dew. He rubbed the dew thoroughly onto his hands. Sure enough, his hands looked cleaner than ever before. "Just wait," he thought, "those girls will be surprised. I will easily win this contest."

During the next day at school, each of the friends hid his or her hands from one another, so that no one could get a peek. When school was finally over, they all walked to the corner. When Brady gave the

signal, they all pulled their hands out from behind their backs. Each friend was very surprised at how clean everyone's hands were.

Just then, an old lady came by dressed in ragged clothes and carrying a dirty, beat-up suitcase. None of them wanted to ask her to be the judge. The lady stopped and looked at the children. "Would one of you youngsters help me with my suitcase?" she asked. "It is very heavy and I must hurry and catch the train."

Each of the young people pretended not to hear the elderly woman. They kept their backs toward her. Finally, Kayla turned and said, "Well, I'm not going that way, but I will help." So Kayla picked-up the heavy suitcase. She and the old lady started to walk down the street.

After they had gone just a few steps, the strangest thing happened. The old lady seemed to turn into the loveliest of angels. She placed her hands on Kayla's head and said, "Kayla has the most attractive hands. The hands that help others are always the nicest."

CHAT BOX

1. Why didn't the children want the old lady to judge their hands?

2. Is it how we look or what we do that makes us beautiful?

3. Do you think that someone can be both ugly and beautiful at the same time? Explain.

Delbert Duck

There once was a wild duck named Delbert. He lived in a lake region in Canada with thousands of other ducks. When the cold winds of fall began to blow, the ducks decided it was time to leave their home in the north and fly south for the winter. Like a great hoard of seaplanes, Delbert and all the other ducks took off from their home on the lake and headed out on their long, hard journey southward.

After traveling for about five hundred miles, Delbert noticed a farm below. Most of the ducks on the farm looked just like him. They were waddling around and eating grain to their heart's content. Delbert let out a loud quack to get the attention of his friend, James. "Look down, James!" Delbert said. "Those ducks are eating like kings

14

while we're flapping our wings off to fly south. All the food we need is right here!"

"Don't be foolish, Delbert," said James. "Those are tame ducks. They don't have the freedom that we have." Delbert turned and looked at his flock then looked back down at the ducks below. "James, I'm going to stay here this winter and take advantage of eating three square meals per day. I'll join up with you again when you return in the spring."

In spite of the warnings James gave, Delbert folded his wings tightly to his side and began diving like an airplane down to the meadow below. Within a few minutes, he began to eat grain with all the other tame ducks.

The days, weeks, and months passed by. Spring came and the ground began to thaw. Everyday Delbert kept watch for James and his buddies to return from the south. He could hardly wait to tell them about the wonderful winter he'd spent.

Early one morning, the sound of quacking ducks awakened Delbert. He looked up to see James and his pals coming in the distance. He quickly said goodbye to his tame friends and got ready for take-off. He began to flap his wings and waddle down the grassy runway. Something was seriously wrong. Delbert's wings had become weak

 15

from lack of exercise and his body was too heavy to lift off the ground. His buddies were now flying overhead and poor Delbert was desperate, for he was eager to join them. He tried once again to take off, flapping and waddling as hard as  he could. It was no use. Poor Delbert couldn't lift off. James circled overhead a few times, shook his head sadly, and then headed north without him.

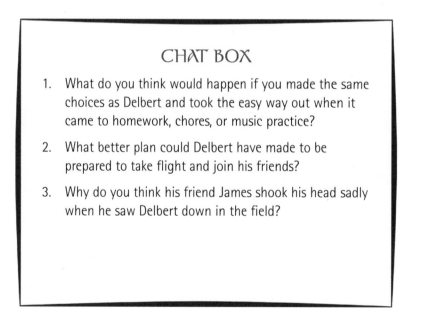

CHAT BOX

1. What do you think would happen if you made the same choices as Delbert and took the easy way out when it came to homework, chores, or music practice?

2. What better plan could Delbert have made to be prepared to take flight and join his friends?

3. Why do you think his friend James shook his head sadly when he saw Delbert down in the field?

The Prince and the Statue

There is an old legend that tells of a prince who had a crooked back. The prince was hunched over whenever he walked or stood. He was a very kind and honorable prince who was well liked by all the people who knew him. However, the prince was extremely disappointed that his appearance and posture were not all that they could be. Many times he would walk through the streets of town and hear people whispering, "Poor Prince Christian, he is such a caring and honest young man. It is a shame about his back."

One day he called a most skillful sculptor to come to his regal home. "I would like you to sculpt a statue of me. I want it full-sized but with a straight back — one that has perfect posture and stands proud. I want to see myself as I might have been."

The sculptor worked long and hard on the statue. He very much wanted to please the prince. At last he was done and it was unveiled for the prince. The completed statue of Prince Christian was so magnificent that his friends suggested placing it at the palace gate. He refused. Instead, he ordered that it be placed in a secret nook in the palace garden where only he could see it.

Day after day the prince visited the garden, staring long and earnestly at the replica of himself. He so loved and admired the marble image that stood straight and proud. Each time he visited, he felt something cause his blood to tingle and his heart to throb.

Months passed. The prince walked through town and heard whispers of a different sort. People could be heard remarking, "The prince seems nobler looking. His back does not seem as crooked."

Hearing this, Prince Christian went back to his garden and stood before the statue. There was no mistaking; his back had become as straight as the statue's and his brow just as noble. The prince had become what he loved and desired.

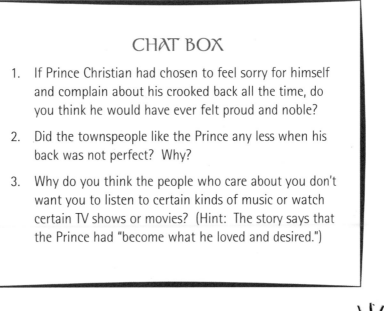

Prince Christian had learned one of the basic laws of life – the possibility to transform into what we idolize, love, and worship.

CHAT BOX

1. If Prince Christian had chosen to feel sorry for himself and complain about his crooked back all the time, do you think he would have ever felt proud and noble?

2. Did the townspeople like the Prince any less when his back was not perfect? Why?

3. Why do you think the people who care about you don't want you to listen to certain kinds of music or watch certain TV shows or movies? (Hint: The story says that the Prince had "become what he loved and desired.")

Troubles

Back in the 1600's, there lived a great English poet who wrote a story about a "mountain of misery." He described how in Greek mythology the ancient and most powerful god, Jupiter, became very upset over the amount of whining and complaining people were doing. So he issued a proclamation to all the people to gather up their problems and miseries. He then ordered everyone to throw their miseries into a gigantic pile in an open field.

All kinds of people, young and old, women and men, brought troubles of every variety. Some people brought their diseases, and others brought their poverty. One woman brought her husband and put him on the pile. Likewise, others put a variety of disagreeable relatives and neighbors. The pile was so full of troubles and misery it almost reached the sky.

When the pile was complete, Jupiter spoke again. He ordered that each person who brought a misery must now take another problem from the pile in place of the one he had given up. Although the people did not like this, it was hard to disobey Jupiter. Each person reluctantly made his choice until all the troubles were redistributed.

The people became an extremely sorry sight! Many of them were frowning and some were crying. They filled the plains with all their complaints and were unhappier than before. Jupiter took pity on the people and allowed each one to take back his own rightful burden — that is, the same problem he had brought to the "mountain of misery."

Jupiter was not such a bad god. He sent out the goddess Patience to help the people. She taught them how to adjust their loads and carry them in an easier manner. Soon they were living a little easier with their own troubles. Each one was very glad that he or she did not have someone else's problem!

CHAT BOX

1. What trouble would you have brought to the mountain of misery?

2. Would you choose to trade your problems for someone else's?

3. Jupiter sent the goddess Patience to help the people. Why are the people happier now that they have "patience" in their lives?

4. Does it help to complain and become unhappy about every problem that comes our way? Explain.

Better than Gold

An old legend tells of a messenger who was sent to a jewel merchant named Dama. Dama was known to have the finest jewels that money could buy. The messenger was seeking to buy Dama's most prized gems for the breastplate of the high priest in Jerusalem.

Dama let the man in and showed him some of his finest jewels. "Are these jewels the very best you have?" asked the messenger. "No sir," replied Dama. "My finest are in a cabinet in my father's room. I will get them for you." Dama left the room and the man anxiously waited to see the treasures that Dama would offer him for sale.

 23

Dama returned after a moment without any jewels to show the messenger. "Where are the jewels?" the messenger asked. Dama explained that his father was feeling ill and that he did not want to disturb him. "We must wait until my father awakens, Sir."

The messenger seemed quite impatient. "I am in a hurry, young man, if you will simply wake up your father, I will buy your jewels and make you very rich."

Dama answered, "My father is not well. Because he is ill he often has trouble sleeping. When he does fall asleep, I do not want to deprive him of his much needed rest. He is much dearer to me than gold or the promise of riches."

So the messenger bowed to Dama and departed without saying more and without buying any jewels. He reported to the high priest that Dama's courtesy to his father was rarer than any gem he had ever seen.

The high priest was so impressed with this report that he went to visit Dama personally. Over time he became Dama's best customer.

CHAT BOX

1. Why did Dama pass up an opportunity to become rich?
2. Why did the messenger bow to Dama?
3. Why do you think that the messenger called Dama's courtesy toward his father "rarer than any gem?"
4. Are there people in your life whom you love and respect more than all the riches on earth? Have you told them?

"Two" Save a Life

Many years ago, a young boy had dreams of becoming a medical doctor. His father was a gardener of a large estate in Scotland, and so there was little or no money available for all the schooling that was needed to become a doctor. Likely, he would end up being a gardener just like his father. It was an honorable job, but not what he wanted.

One weekend the owners of the estate invited some guests over for rest and relaxation. One boy jumped into the swimming pool and was suddenly stricken with cramps. His cries were loud enough for the gardener's son to hear. As the boy began sinking, the gardener's son jumped into the water and dragged the drowning boy to safety. Deeply moved by this act of bravery, the parents of the boy asked to see the gardener.

"We are deeply grateful, Sir, what can we do to reward your son?" asked the parents. "We want no reward," said the gardener, "we're only glad that our son could swim and was prepared for the emergency." After a few moments and some additional questions, the gardener shared the story of his son's dream to become a doctor. The visitors exclaimed, "That's it! We will see that your son's entire education is provided for."

And that they did. They carried out the promise they had made that day. The gardener's son became one of the world's greatest physicians, Dr. Alexander Fleming. He is best known for discovering the wonder drug penicillin. The boy whom he had saved also became one of the great world leaders of the last century, Winston Churchill.

Long after the swimming pool incident, while making a trip to Egypt, Winston Churchill became seriously ill with pneumonia. At that time he was the Prime Minister of Great Britain and was greatly needed by his country. Although his advisors had given up hope for his recovery, a hurried call was sent out to Scotland for Dr. Alexander Fleming. He was quickly flown in and sent to the bedside of Mr. Churchill. He brought a precious container of penicillin with him and gave the miracle drug to his patient. Winston Churchill recovered from the illness and was able to resume his duties.

Now you know the true story of how one man was able to save another person's life not once, but twice.

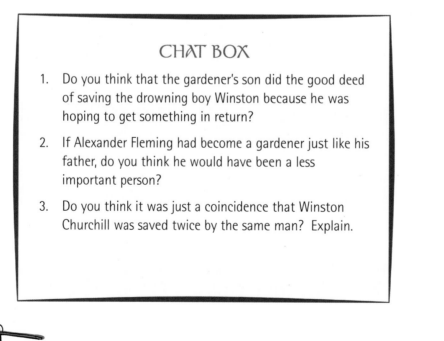

CHAT BOX

1. Do you think that the gardener's son did the good deed of saving the drowning boy Winston because he was hoping to get something in return?

2. If Alexander Fleming had become a gardener just like his father, do you think he would have been a less important person?

3. Do you think it was just a coincidence that Winston Churchill was saved twice by the same man? Explain.

The Piano Lesson

Professor Bridger was a famous music teacher who loved to collect old pianos. A few years ago, the Professor and his wife bought a very old and special piano at a yard sale. This piano was so unique that they decided to put it in their living room.

One evening, late at night, Professor Bridger was feeling famished. He got out of bed to get a bite to eat. When he went into the kitchen, he began to hear voices. His wife was upstairs sleeping and so he thought it must be his neighbors. But, he soon realized that the voices were coming from his own living room! There was not a soul in the room, yet he could hear an argument taking place. To his amazement, he realized that the keys on his piano were talking, and most of the talk was not very nice.

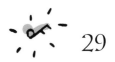

One of the keys seemed to be leading the discussion. It was the big note, G. He was quite loud, boastful, obnoxious and somewhat of a bully. "You know, you guys are not very important," he said. I could make most of this music by myself." He

began to play and talk loud because he wanted everyone to know he was there, and how important he was.

When G finished showing off, little C note began speaking. She seemed quite sad and discouraged. "Well, I guess you're right, Mr. G," she said, "you don't need me at all. I'm just too small to be of much use." These thoughts made her so unhappy, she began to cry.

The other notes began to play and argue at the same time, but poor little C note was crying so hard that she didn't even try.

Professor Bridger sat in his big overstuffed chair and wondered how the argument between the keys would turn out. Would all the keys become upset and quit playing or, perhaps, would some rebel and refuse to play with the others? He noticed that the music didn't sound very good at all without little C note.

Suddenly, A note spoke up. He sounded very upset by all the fuss. "This is nonsense!" he said. "We must have an end to all this foolishness. If we are ever to have harmony, we must all work

30

together!" The other notes began to listen carefully, even big G note. "Each one of us has an important part to play," continued A note, "no matter how big or small we may seem. Let's get to work and let's cooperate!"

Professor Bridger was pleased with the outcome of the discussion between the piano keys. They began to play all together, creating beautiful music, each note adding its own special voice. Not only did the piano remind the Professor of the power of working together as a team, the music also helped him fall fast asleep in his big overstuffed chair.

Of course, he forgot all about his hunger.

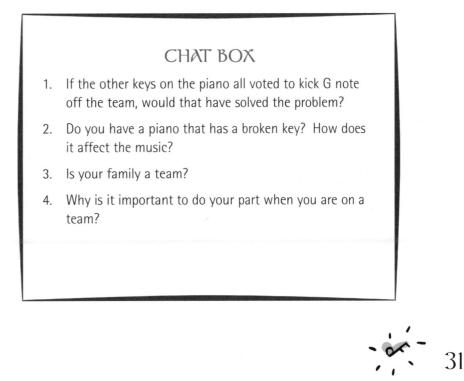

CHAT BOX

1. If the other keys on the piano all voted to kick G note off the team, would that have solved the problem?

2. Do you have a piano that has a broken key? How does it affect the music?

3. Is your family a team?

4. Why is it important to do your part when you are on a team?

Reflecting Greatness

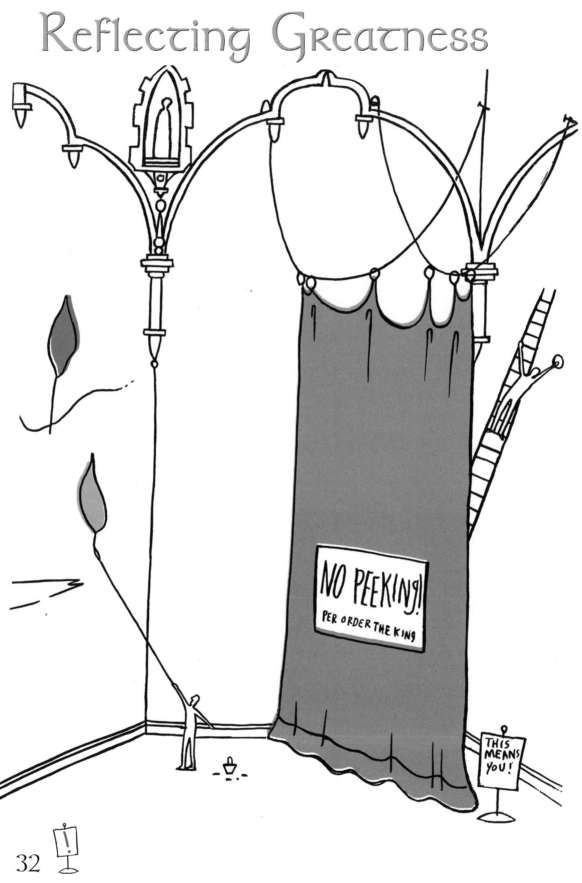

Many centuries ago, a king lived in a great palace. It was amazingly beautiful. However, there was one room that was not as nice as all the rest. In fact, it was quite drab. The large, narrow banquet room did not have enough color or brightness. The king did not like this room and so he decided to do something about the walls. "I will have a contest and award a prize to the one who paints the most beautiful picture," said the king.

The king's men went in search throughout the land for the two most talented artists. They returned with two men, one many years younger than the other. The king had them placed together in the spacious but narrow banquet room and there they were provided with all the paints they could ever want or need. A large curtain was stretched between them so that neither artist would see what the other was creating.

For several weeks the artists worked in the room, hardly taking time to eat or sleep. Finally the day arrived when the contest was to end.

A trumpet was blown and the curtain was lowered. The king stood in utter amazement. Each wall displayed the exact same mural! "How is this possible?" he asked. Every detail was identical.

When the king walked up to take a closer look at the wall, he discovered the secret. The younger of the artists had done nothing but polish his wall so that it became a giant mirror, reflecting the work of the other artist. When the man was asked why he had polished instead of painted, he answered, "I knew that if I could polish the wall enough so that it would reflect the magnificent talent of my friend, I would be satisfied. I wanted no prize. I am pleased to know that I helped reflect his greatness."

The king was so pleased and surprised by the noble actions of the young man that he awarded prizes to both of them.

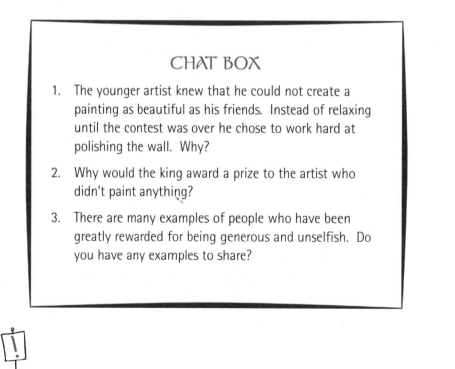

CHAT BOX

1. The younger artist knew that he could not create a painting as beautiful as his friends. Instead of relaxing until the contest was over he chose to work hard at polishing the wall. Why?

2. Why would the king award a prize to the artist who didn't paint anything?

3. There are many examples of people who have been greatly rewarded for being generous and unselfish. Do you have any examples to share?

The Wise Woman and the Bird

There once was a wise woman who lived in a little shack on the edge of town. She was so wise that people came from all over the world to ask her questions. They always received the right answers and usually found the answers very helpful.

In this town, there also lived a mean-spirited young girl. She was a showoff and liked to find fault with other people. She did not like the wise woman. She was not pleased with how kind and compassionate the old woman was and how the woman knew the answers to everyone's questions.

The girl decided that she would embarrass the wise woman by proving her wrong. She planned to find a small bird, hold it in her hands, and ask the woman if it was alive or dead. If the wise woman told her it was living, she would squeeze her hands and show that the bird was dead. If the wise woman said that the bird was dead, she would open her hands and show that it was alive.

The young girl quickly found a tiny bird and caught it in her hands. She went to the wise woman and asked, "Wise Woman, is the tiny bird in my hands alive or dead?" The wise woman did not look at the girl's hands; instead, she gazed deep into the young girl's eyes.

 35

Quietly the wise woman replied, "My dear young lady, it is up to you whether or not the little bird lives or dies. You are totally responsible for every aspect of your life and only you can decide whether to be cruel or whether to be kind to that bird. The right to make good choices is always there if you decide to look for it."

Once again, the wise woman was right and the girl was deeply moved by this answer. The girl used to believe the same thing but somehow this belief had been lost. She had forgotten how to be responsible and loving. The young girl found that she no longer hated the wise woman. She quickly decided to let the bird go free.

The girl learned another valuable lesson – happiness comes from making kind and compassionate decisions. The wise woman had helped her see the value of goodness.

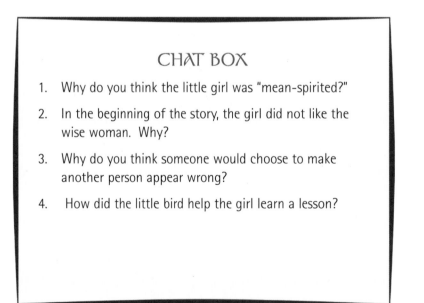

CHAT BOX

1. Why do you think the little girl was "mean-spirited?"

2. In the beginning of the story, the girl did not like the wise woman. Why?

3. Why do you think someone would choose to make another person appear wrong?

4. How did the little bird help the girl learn a lesson?

A Bell for the Cat

Once in an old house there lived a large family of mice. They all got along quite well together. Unfortunately for the mice, there also lived a cat in the same house. The mice were afraid of the cat, for he was quick and quiet and often hungry. Whenever a mouse ventured out, he was in danger of being captured by the furry feline.

The mice were very careful and would send out messages to one another about the cat's location. Several mice would sneak out for food while the cat was in the other side of the house. One day grandfather mouse said, "This is terrible. We are always living in constant fear for our lives. Our stomachs are tied up in knots, making it difficult to eat, and we can barely sleep at night. I am so nervous that I can't even fall asleep in church anymore!"

The grandfather mouse waited for a time when the family cat took a trip in the car with his owners. He called together all the mice in the house for a grand mouse meeting. "We must figure out a solution to our cat problem! We have already lost many of our family members to the hungry cat," he pleaded. "We simply cannot live like this anymore. Ideas from all mice are welcome."

Many ideas were discussed and shared between the mice. Some of them sounded pretty good. Others were quite bad.

One of the younger mice made the prize suggestion. "I say we tie a bell around the cat's neck. Then when we hear 'ting-a-ling ting-a-ling,' we'll have plenty of time to hide." That was the best idea any mouse ears could hear! The young mouse was picked up and placed on the shoulders of the other mice and paraded around the room. There were plans for a huge celebration. Surely this was the solution to their problem.

When the excitement and shouting had died down and the mice had returned to their seats, a great grandmother mouse stood up and took a few steps forward. "I've watched all of this with great interest and even shared in the excitement of this new idea," she said, "but I do believe that we have overlooked one very important thing. Who is going to tie the bell around the cat's neck?"

None of the other mice had considered that question. No one was eager to take on the dangerous assignment. All the mice quietly left their seats and tiptoed out of the room. Each was afraid that he or she might be asked to volunteer. The excitement was gone and they were all terribly disappointed.

CHAT BOX

1. Having family discussions can be a productive way to solve problems. Do you think that both the older family members and the younger should be able to share their thoughts during important discussions?

2. Often there are times in our lives when we come up with incredible ideas. Is coming up with a wonderful idea enough to make a difference?

3. It takes discipline, courage and hard work to follow through with good ideas. Do you have an idea that you are willing to work hard at in order to make it happen?

A Real Champion

One morning many years ago, two young boys left early for their little country school. They had quite a long walk through the snow. It was their turn to light the fire in the big stove so that the children could be warm when school started. Floyd, one of the boys, grabbed what he thought was a can of coal oil and poured the contents freely on the wood. When he struck the match, there was an explosion. The school building immediately caught fire and burned to the ground. Floyd had accidentally poured gasoline on the wood. He was killed in the fire. His friend Glenn was so badly injured that no one believed he would ever walk again.

Glenn was bedridden and unable to move for several weeks. The toes on his left foot were almost gone and his right leg was crooked. The young boy gazed at his frail wobbly legs and wondered if they would ever again allow him to run and play.

Members of Glenn's family were very caring and took turns massaging his legs. After several years, he was able to walk again. He couldn't walk steadily or rapidly, but he could walk just enough to get along. Time passed and he became stronger. He began to run. He loved running with his school friends across the wide expanse of the fields in Kansas. And at fourteen, he entered his first race, a mile run at the local fair. He was the winner.

When Glenn attended the University of Kansas, in 1932, he was sent to Los Angeles to represent his state in the trials for the Olympic

41

Games. He won the mile race in four minutes and fourteen seconds. The audience roared with excitement. One hour later he returned to the track and won the half-mile championship in one minute and fifty-three and one-half seconds. Later in his career, he broke both of those records and established a world record!

One time, after Glenn had won a great race, his hometown celebrated in the streets with confetti and streamers. When the celebration was over, Glenn got into some old clothes and helped his dad, the town's street cleaner, sweep up the litter.

Glenn Cunningham was one of our country's most popular sports heroes. He was helpful and modest. He was seldom without pain but didn't complain about it. His difficulties seemed to make him more determined to succeed. His name is honored in all countries where people admire courage, determination, and good sportsmanship.

CHAT BOX

1. Glenn had legs that were badly injured yet he broke the world's record in running. How do you think he was able to accomplish this feat?

2. This true story tells about how Glenn helped his father clean the streets after a huge party given in his honor. Would you be willing to help your parents clean the house after your birthday party?

3. Some people just talk about what they want to do, others just do it. What do you think helped Glenn become so determined to be an Olympic runner?

Jakob's Valley

Long ago, there was a land called Jakob's Valley. It was incredibly lush and beautiful. There has never been another like it since.

Jakob's Valley was part of a kingdom that was filled with thousands of fruit trees. Most of the people who lived there took pride in making the best fruit juices on earth. Many of them had a special cellar to store their most prized juices in. Some turned their juices into wine. Wine collectors from all over the world coveted the wines from Jakob's Valley.

The king and queen of the kingdom decided to have a great feast in celebration of their wonderful land and all the bountiful fruits it produced. They put out a request to all the citizens to come to the gala, bringing a bottle of their very best wine for the occasion.

43

An invitation to the palace was a rare event. The excitement could be felt throughout the valley. Not a soul wanted to miss out on the festivities.

On the day of the feast, hundreds of people crowded into the palace. Each guest reached up to pour the contents of his or her bottle into the giant container made especially for the occasion. Everyone was anxious to share the exquisite flavors which their valley produced.

The feast began. The tap on the container was opened and the glasses were filled. Suddenly, there was a look of surprise on everyone's face. The glasses had only water in them - not fine wine. Unfortunately, each of the guests had believed that everyone else would bring fine wine and so decided to fill his own bottle with just water. Each had assumed that his single bottle of water would not weaken the fine wine that everyone else had brought.

The celebration turned out to be a huge disappointment to the king, queen, and all of the guests. What could have been a most wonderful occasion instead became diluted by selfishness and greed.

CHAT BOX

1. When we don't give our best, or give less than we could, how does it affect those around us?

2. Sometimes it is not easy to give away something that is special to us, even though we may be rewarded with good feelings or memories. Do you think the guests might have done things differently had they known the party would be ruined?

3. There are many people who choose to give away something special on a regular basis – their time. They volunteer in schools, churches, and community service. Do you think this type of person would have brought water or wine to the Jakob's Valley celebration?

Ordinary Brown Packages

Many years ago, the manager of one of the world's richest diamond mines made an astonishing discovery. As he invited some visitors into the mine, he stopped in amazement. At their feet lay what looked to be a large sparkling diamond. At first he thought it could not be possible. "It must be a broken bottle," he thought. Upon closer examination, he realized it truly was a brilliant diamond, the largest one ever found in the mine and worth a fortune.

Immediately the question arose as to how such a large and priceless diamond would be transported from Africa to England where it could be sold. A plan was soon devised. Four husky men, heavily armed with guns, were given a securely wrapped package and started on their journey. They had to walk sixty miles through the jungle in order to reach the railroad. During that time the men worked in shifts. As two of them rested, the other two kept their eyes on the package and a lookout for problems. They knew that they were in continual danger of robbers, for already the entire world had heard of the discovery of the diamond.

When they reached the railroad, a special car was waiting to transport them to the coast. When they reached the shore they boarded a ship to England. Upon arriving, the men were met by another high security train that brought them into London where they were to deliver the little box.

The great moment arrived. The package was to be opened by the diamond company president. Policemen surrounded the building. Inside, everyone stood on the tips of their toes to get the first glimpse of the great diamond. When the box was finally unwrapped, there, to everyone's utter surprise, was nothing but a chunk of coal. Where was the precious diamond? Had the manager of the mine stolen the real diamond and sent only this piece of coal?

The room was filled with excited and upset people. They must hurry and capture the manager before it was too late! Just as they were deciding what to do, there came a knock at the door. The crowd gathered to see who it was. The door was opened and there stood the mailman. He handed the president a plain looking package and said, "It's for you, Sir." It was an ordinary cardboard box, wrapped in brown paper and tied with ordinary string. The president took the box and opened it. Everyone in the room was astounded to see that inside the ordinary box was the sparkling diamond from the African mine.

The little box was safely sent from the jungles of Africa, over land and sea, by way of the post office. Because no one was aware of the value of the contents of the brown paper package, it was overlooked and ignored.

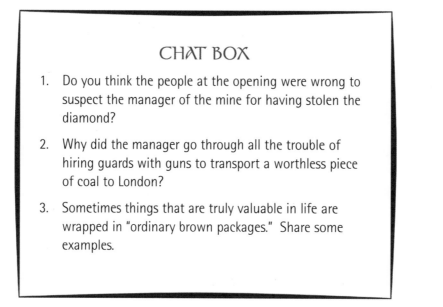

CHAT BOX

1. Do you think the people at the opening were wrong to suspect the manager of the mine for having stolen the diamond?

2. Why did the manager go through all the trouble of hiring guards with guns to transport a worthless piece of coal to London?

3. Sometimes things that are truly valuable in life are wrapped in "ordinary brown packages." Share some examples.

The Antelope and the Spider

There once was an antelope who lived in Africa. One day a fire had started in the tall grass. As the antelope began to run, she heard a small voice that cried, "Save me! Save me!" The antelope turned to listen and find where the tiny voice was coming from. Next to a dry leaf by her hoof, she noticed a spider. Again, the small voice cried out to the antelope. "Oh please, would you carry me away from the fire? My legs are too short. I won't be able run fast enough to escape."

The antelope asked herself whether or not it was worth risking her life in order to carry one little spider to safety. Again she heard another plea from the spider. "If you will save me, I will help you one day."

The antelope laughed and asked the spider, "What could a tiny, insignificant thing like you do for a big animal like me?" The spider replied, "I don't know yet, Ms. Antelope, but someday I will help you when you are in need."

The antelope gave in to the spider's plea and told him to climb up her leg and crawl onto her back, "Hold on between my horns so that you won't fall off when I run." The spider let out a delightful squeal and hopped onto her back. The antelope ran very fast. The spider and the antelope safely escaped the fire.

A few weeks later, the antelope heard dogs and hunters coming after her. The vicious dogs were getting closer and closer. She was fearful that the hunters would find her and kill her. Suddenly she heard the spider call out. "I'll save you!" he shouted. "How can you help me? You are just a tiny bug!" cried the frightened antelope. "Hide in the grass and I'll show you!" he instructed. The antelope leaped behind a patch of very tall grass.

The spider frantically began weaving his silver webs over each of the antelope's footprints. The antelope was shaking in her hiding place as the hunters came near. One of them looked down at the footprints and angrily shouted, "These tracks are at least two days old! There are spider webs all over them. She didn't go this way!" The hunters turned around and

began to hike in the opposite direction. The spider's sigh of relief was almost as loud as the antelope's.

And so the tiny spider saved the big antelope. The antelope realized that no matter how small or insignificant one may seem, he or she may still have the ability to make an important difference.

CHAT BOX

1. What did you learn from this story?

2. Why did the antelope save the spider even though she didn't believe that the spider could return the favor?

3. Do you sometimes feel small and insignificant?

4. Do you know anyone else who might feel small and unimportant? Think about sharing this story with him or her.

The Boy Who Made Soap

In the 1800's, a sixteen year old boy named William left home with a small bundle that contained everything he owned, including homemade soap, a tooth brush and tooth cleanser. With a sparkle in his eyes, he headed for the big city of New York to find a job. On the way, he ran into a friend of the family. When the old man found out where the boy was going, he said, "Be sure you start out right, Lad, and you will get along fine." "Thank you," said William, "but the only thing I know how to do, Sir, is make soap and candles."

Being a spiritual man who cared for William, he knelt down in the open air and began to pray that his young friend would be guided and taken care of while in the big city.

After he prayed, he gave William some advice. "Someone will soon be the leading soap maker in New York. It can be you as well as anyone else. Continue to be a decent man, and live a clean life by making the right choices. Give back something from every dollar you make and you will be a rich man – if not in money, then in joy.

When William arrived in New York he found a place to stay and began to look for work. Remembering the words of his friend, he tried hard to make the right choices. He finally got his first job and worked hard. William always gave a portion of his wages to the church and other worthy charities.

Because of William's continued self-discipline, he secured a better job. Eventually he became a partner in a soap business. Years went by and finally William became the owner of the business that was eventually known as the "Colgate Company." Under William's direction the company grew and prospered. Today the Colgate name continues as part of a company known as Colgate Palmolive. It is nearly impossible to go into a store today without seeing some sort of "foaming," "cleaning" or "brightening" product by the Colgate Palmolive Company on the shelves.

William never forgot his old friend's advice about "giving back" to others. And just like bubble bath under running water, his business grew and grew and he gave more and more money to those in need. He was able to pay for all of his family's needs and still give away almost 40% of his earnings. Some might call that "filthy rich," but there was nothing dirty about his business!

William Colgate was someone who was crystal clear about his goals and dedicated himself to building a worthwhile business and helping those who were poor and downtrodden. Not only did his generosity feed his own soul and spirit, but along with his self-discipline and love for his work, he was able to become a very wealthy man.

CHAT BOX

1. Why is self-discipline so important?

2. When you buy toothpaste or soap and see "Colgate" on the packaging, what will you remember most about the man responsible for the Colgate Palmolive Company's success?

3. William obviously believed that we were given one hand to receive with and another to give with. Someone once said that "not giving back would be like wearing a catcher's mitt on each hand." Explain.

4. What do you think is meant by the following saying: "We make a living by what we get. We make a life by what we give."

Old Dog Tray

There once was an old dog named Tray. He was big and burly with long, multicolored hair that was matted into many small patches. Tray sometimes had problems getting up after a long doggie nap, but he still had it in him to run fast when he wanted to.

One day, while Tray was wandering through the forest with his owner, he caught sight of a huge black bear. Tray was fearless. And, although the bear was far bigger than he was, Tray knew that he could catch the big beast. So, Tray jetted into the woods in rapid pursuit.

Suddenly, a large, white wolf crossed Tray's path. Tray immediately lost interest in his race with the bear and began chasing the wolf. The wolf, on her way back home to check on her cubs, moved swiftly

55

and silently through the woods. Tray, barking furiously as he ran, nearly caught up to her when he saw something else leap from a pile of old logs. It was a fox who was startled from his den. Tray's attention was diverted, once again. The old dog took another turn and, with matted hair flopping about, he tore after the streak of red fur ahead of him. The sly fox darted here and there and then ran in a large circle. Finally the fox ran through some thick bushes and back into his den.

As the fox ran through the bushes he frightened a rabbit that began to hop rapidly down the path. Tray caught sight of the rabbit and quickly left the fox chase. He started after the rabbit and, even though he was beginning to get tired and thirsty, convinced himself that he was the master hunter and could catch anything he wanted. Tray was gaining steadily on the rabbit. The tired bunny almost gave up. He began to believe that the dog would catch him, and that he would never again see his bunny wife and his baby bunnies. Lucky for

him, however, the old dog noticed a small squirrel running down a tree and onto the path. Once again, Tray took his eyes off of what he was chasing and began running after something new – the squirrel.

The squirrel squeaked in fright and ran as fast as she could. Tray dashed toward her but she quickly ran up a different tree and rested on a high branch safely out of Tray's reach. The squirrel scolded and scolded. Tray ended up barking and barking at a squirrel high in an old elm tree. With a face full of slobber, aching doggie legs, and pure exhaustion, he plopped himself onto a hill of pine needles. He was hungry, thirsty and tired. His eyes began to get heavy as he wondered why his efforts were unsuccessful.

Poor old dog, Tray! If only he hadn't become distracted by so many different things. First he wanted to catch the bear, then the wolf, then the fox, then the rabbit, then the squirrel. But, he never caught any of them.

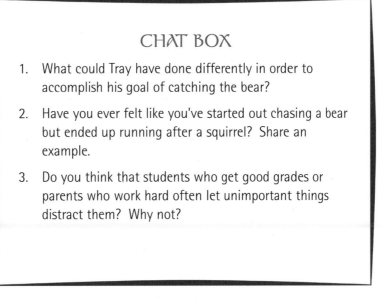

CHAT BOX

1. What could Tray have done differently in order to accomplish his goal of catching the bear?

2. Have you ever felt like you've started out chasing a bear but ended up running after a squirrel? Share an example.

3. Do you think that students who get good grades or parents who work hard often let unimportant things distract them? Why not?

The Magic Mask

There once was a great and powerful ruler named King Cedric III. He had a very large kingdom and ruled over thousands of soldiers. He was brave and fearless; respected by all. But, he loved no one and no one loved him. Without love he became more and more lonely. His face reflected the bitterness and unhappiness in his life. There were deep, ugly lines around his cruel-looking mouth. He never smiled. A frown was permanently furrowed in his forehead.

In one of King Cedric's cities, there lived a beautiful woman. The king had often watched her as she walked around the marketplace. She always showed kindness and concern for everyone she met. The ruler fell in love with her and wanted to make her his wife. He dressed in his finest royal robes and placed his jeweled crown upon his head. He looked in his mirror to see what sort of picture he would present to the radiant, caring woman. He saw nothing but a cruel, hard face that he feared would cause dislike in the lady he loved.

King Cedric had the sudden notion to send for a magician. "Make me a mask of the thinnest wax that will follow my features. I want you to paint it with your magic paints so that I will look kind and pleasant. Fasten it upon my face so that I will never have to take it off. And, of course, make it handsome. Use your greatest skill and I will pay you whatever price you ask."

"This I can do," said the magician, "on one condition. You must keep your face in the same lines which I paint on the mask or it will be ruined forever and I will not be able to replace it."

"I will do anything you say," said the ruler eagerly, "anything to win the love and admiration of this woman. But tell me how do I keep the mask from cracking?"

"You must think kindly thoughts," replied the magician. "And to do this, you must do kindly deeds. You must make your kingdom

 59

peaceful as well as powerful. You must replace anger with understanding and love. Be gracious and courteous to all."

So the magnificent mask was made. No one could see that it was not the true face of the king. He now appeared brave and fearless as well as handsome, kind and loving. Months passed by and, although the mask was in danger of ruin, the man fought hard to keep his face in the kindly form that was painted for him.

Eventually the lovely woman became his bride. His people believed that a miracle had happened. They credited the king's wife for his new kindness. They said that her good qualities had rubbed off on him.

Since gentleness and thoughtfulness had entered the life of King Cedric, decency and honesty were his too. Soon, however, the king began to worry. He regretted having deceived his loyal and caring wife with the magic mask.

At last he could no longer tolerate it and called for the magician. "Remove this false mask! It is not my true self," he cried. "My wife and my subjects deserve to know the truth!"

"If I do," warned the magician, "I can never make another one for you and you must always wear your own face for as long as you live."

"Better that," said the king, "than to live dishonestly."

The magician took off the ruler's mask. The king swiftly picked up his mirror. To his surprise, his eyes had brightened, his lips were curved into a smile, and the ugly lines were gone. His frown had disappeared. His face was the exact likeness of the mask he had worn for so long.

When the king returned to his wife, she noticed nothing unusual. She simply saw the familiar features of the man she loved – a man who had become kind, honest and loving.

CHAT BOX

1. Why did the magician tell King Cedric III that he needed to behave kindly to others?

2. If ugly thoughts and deeds create an ugly appearance, why do you think that some people choose to be angry and miserable?

3. Why did the king choose to take off his mask?

4. Do you think his wife would have been upset with him if the king had told her about the mask before removing it? Why, or why not?

5. Do you think that your face looks better when you are angry and unhappy or when you are kind and joyful?

The Glowing Painting

In 1826, an artist named Joseph Turner entered his painting in an art exhibit. The scene was the German city of Cologne. He painted the golden sky in such a way that the whole picture seemed to glow and come alive. It was a magnificent and extraordinary piece of art. Mr. Turner's painting was by far the winning entry in the exhibit.

Another artist, named Sir Thomas Lawrence, also entered a couple of paintings in the exhibit. Sir Thomas' paintings were placed on either side of Mr. Turner's radiant painting. Sir Thomas' work now seemed to be quite colorless and drab in comparison. He was not pleased with where the exhibit manager had hung his paintings. He complained and requested that his paintings be moved to another location on the wall.

There was a rule at the exhibition that artists were not allowed to move their artwork once it had been put on display. They were, however, permitted to make finishing touches.

On the morning of the exhibition, Mr. Turner's friends were anxious to see his masterpiece, "Cologne." They had heard about its spectacular gleaming quality. They eagerly approached the much talked-about masterpiece. How astounded they were to see that the picture they had heard so much about was actually very dreary and lifeless! It had a dull, lackluster, gray cast to it and was not at all "glowing." It was obviously not very good! It was apparent that someone had tampered with it. One of Mr. Turner's friends was alarmed and turned to him and asked, "What in the world happened to your picture?"

With a smile, Mr. Turner whispered to his friend the entire story of Sir Thomas Lawrence's complaint about the placement of his artwork at the exhibit. At length, Mr. Turner explained, "Poor Sir Thomas was so unhappy, I decided to put some finishing touches on my own painting. It is only some lamp black and it will all wash off after the exhibition."

The famous landscape artist, Joseph Turner, who entered his first exhibit at age fifteen, had ruined his own picture for the time of the exhibition by brushing a wash of lamp black over the splendor of the once "glowing" canvas. In so doing, Mr. Turner was able to make his competitor's paintings stand out and appear far more beautiful than they had when they were first placed next to the untouched "Cologne."

Mr. Turner was one of the great souls of the world who unselfishly gave up something personally valuable to enhance the self-worth of another.

CHAT BOX

1. How easy, or difficult, do you think it would it be for you to help someone else win a contest that you had entered?

2. Is it cheating to help your competitor to win? Explain.

3. Do you think that Sir Thomas Lawrence deserved to have his paintings outshine Joseph Turner's? Why, or why not

The Rainbow Flower

On a lush green mountainside many years ago, legend tells of a shepherd boy named Edward who found a strange and colorful flower. There were seven petals on the flower, each of them a different shade of the rainbow. He quickly knelt down and plucked it from the dewy grass. When he brought it up to his nose to smell its fragrance, he realized that this was no ordinary flower. The aroma was like nothing he had ever smelled before. It was a fragrance that he imagined could only come from Heaven.

As the boy held the flower in his hand, he felt the ground beneath his feet shake. A cave suddenly opened up before him, and strange but wonderful music beckoned to him. He entered the cave and his heart was filled with a feeling of joy that was beyond description. Soft colors of pink and violet began to shimmer; accompanied by the sound of celestial violins. Edward had never ever experienced such a feeling. He thought he was dreaming.

After many hours of enjoying the colors and sounds of that glorious cave, Edward decided to pick up the magical flower and climb back up through the cave to check on his sheep in the pasture. They all looked happy and safe, and so Edward decided to turn around and go back into the cave. This time something was different. The cave had a gigantic stone in front of it.

As the shepherd boy stepped up to the stone, he realized that he was getting quite hungry. While thinking about eating, he took another sniff of the rainbow-colored flower. Immediately the stone in front of the cave shook mightily and began to slide away from the opening. The first thing Edward noticed was the pleasing aroma of food. He slowly entered the cave and found that it looked completely different from the first time. Now the cavern was filled with every kind of food imaginable. There were mashed potatoes, fresh baked pies, fresh steamed vegetables, and rich, tasty sauces everywhere. All of Edward's favorite things to eat were right before his eyes.

Of course, the boy could not resist trying some of the delectable dishes that were sitting before him. He ate and ate until he could eat no more. He picked up the rainbow flower and waddled out of the cave. "Thank you, strange flower," he said.

Once again the shepherd boy went to check on his sheep. While they were doing just fine, Edward had indigestion. Though his belly didn't feel like any more exploring, Edward could not resist walking toward another cave that appeared before him. This one was blocked by a huge stone that glimmered like a diamond. As he walked up to the stone, with the strange flower in his hand, it slowly moved away from the opening. Edward's mouth dropped and he gasped. The

66

cave was filled with sparkling diamonds of every color. They were flawless and radiant, illuminating the whole cavern.

The shepherd boy quickly ran to the diamonds and stuffed every pocket he could fill. When every conceivable space in his clothing was filled with diamonds, he swiftly began to exit the cave. He heard a gentle voice coming from the inside. "Don't forget what is most important!" it said. Seeing the magical flower laying on the floor, he thought, "Who needs a flower when I have all these riches?"

When the boy stepped foot outside of the cave, he had one last glimpse of the flower before the stone began to move and block the opening. The cave disappeared. He began to open his shirt and empty his pockets, only to find that the gleaming diamonds had all turned to dust. The very thing that allowed the boy to experience the most magnificent things in his life was left behind on a cold stone floor in exchange for diamonds that turned to dust.

CHAT BOX

1. How do you think Edward's life might have changed if he had listened to the gentle voice inside the cave advising him to not leave the flower behind?

2. Do you ever hear a voice inside of yourself that helps you to make right decisions?

3. If there is someone, or something, that is responsible for the good things that come into your life, how can you show your appreciation?

Martin of Tours

About 1500 years ago, a young man named Martin became a soldier in the army. Along with many others, he was sent to a city in the northern part of France. The winter he spent there was long and hard. The weather was terribly cold and many poor people died from lack of food and clothing.

One evening, the soldiers returned to the city after a long horseback ride in the country. It was a bitter cold day. The soldiers were clothed in their armor which was covered with a long military cloak. The cloak was made from a large piece of cloth, perfectly round, with an opening in the center for the head.

Near the entrance of the city gate, a beggar stood at the side of the road. He had little clothing and was leaning on a crutch. Shivering from the cold, he held out his hand and asked for a gift. While the other soldiers paid no attention and continued to ride ahead, Martin was moved to help. Unselfish as he was, he had no money left to give the beggar, for he had already given it all away. The great warm military cloak was all he had left.

"This poor man," he thought, "has need of my cloak. If I share it with him, there will be enough to keep both of us warm."

The generous, young soldier took his sword and cut the vast piece of cloth down the middle. Leaning from his horse, Martin wrapped one half of the cloak around the shoulders of the half-frozen man. He put the sword back into his sheath, tossed the other half of the cloak over his own shoulders, and turned his horse to ride after his fellow soldiers. Some of the soldiers had laughed, but the others wished they had been as generous and thoughtful.

As legend tells, the young soldier had a dream that night. He saw the beggar in Heaven wearing the other half of his cloak. "See," he was saying, "what the soldier shared with me? It was half of all that he had."

Martin became one of the greatest men of his time. He was noted for his kindness, generosity, and helpfulness to others. He later became a Bishop in the church and was known as "Martin of Tours." To this day, there are many pictures and statues in France depicting Martin, sword in hand, cutting his cloak to give to a beggar.

CHAT BOX

1. Why do you think some of the soldiers laughed when Martin cut his cloak for the poor beggar?

2. Do you think the beggar appreciated what Martin had done for him? What in the story makes you believe that?

3. What can we do today to be more like Martin of Tours of 1500 years ago?

The Two Apples

One day a young boy named Tyler knocked at the door of Haven, a neighbor and good friend. He was very upset and knew that his older, wiser friend might have something to say to calm his sad heart. Haven was only about two years older but he always seemed to understand.

"Come on in Tyler," said Haven. "What's up?"

Tyler was almost on the verge of tears when he explained to his friend how his older brother had gotten into trouble and been taken away by the police. Tyler grabbed a chair to sit down at the kitchen table while Haven went to the refrigerator to get some cheese to snack on. "Haven," asked Tyler, "why do some kids take the wrong road and get into trouble?"

"Well, Tyler," Haven responded, "my dad has always told me and my brother to take the 'higher' road – the one that calls for us to be honest, and to not listen to our friends when they encourage us to do the wrong thing. This choice frequently requires a little more effort. Often, the easy road will take us down hill."

Tyler was confused. "What do you mean?" he questioned. "My brother definitely went 'down hill' but he is not having an easy time of it."

"Exactly," Haven responded, "Once you get to the bottom, it's that much harder to climb back up."

72

Tyler still seemed puzzled. He was worried that since his own brother had big problems that he, too, might end up in the same place. "He's my brother, Haven! I have aunts and uncles who got into trouble, too. Am I going to end up like them?"

Haven was about to grab one of the apples from the basket on the table. He planned to cut it up and add it to the plate of cheese. Then he paused. "See these two apples?" he said, "They are Macintosh and come from an apple tree in my back yard. They probably grew on the same limb together. In fact, at one time they looked very much alike – shiny skins washed by the rain and dried by the wind.

"Something happened to this one with the big brown spot," he continued. "It is a windfall apple. That is, it blew from the tree during a storm and was bruised and hurt as it hit the ground. The other one I picked from the tree when it was ripe. One survived the storm and the other didn't.

"If the windfall apple could talk, he would probably tell you that the fall caused him more pains than a church's stained glass window. He was meant to remain on the tree until a ripe old age. But he made a big mistake. When he was just a little apple, a worm knocked on his door. He let it come in and live with him. He opened the door so wide that other members of the worm's family came and lived there, too. He got weaker and weaker and when the big wind came, he just couldn't hold on."

Tyler was still a little puzzled. He wasn't real clear as to how the apples and the worms related to his brother being arrested. "So worms came in and started living in my brother's brain?" he asked.

"Well, sort of," laughed Haven, "especially if we think of those worms as being bad thoughts, anger, disrespect and dishonesty." He explained to his friend that it didn't matter what other family members chose to do, he was free to make his own choices. If his friends tried to get him to do something he knew wasn't right, he could take the higher road and not go along. "It may take a little more courage," he said, "but you will avoid a very painful fall."

Tyler was happy that he was able to talk with Haven about his brother and appreciated what his wise friend was trying to tell him. And, Haven was pleased that he could help.

"Have an apple!" said Haven.

Tyler smiled, "Can I have the one without the worms in it?"

CHAT BOX

1. Have your friends ever wanted you to do something that would not be the high road? Is it easier some times to just go along?

2. Some people have family members or friends who don't always make the right choices. Oftentimes they don't realize the trouble and pain that will come. How can we learn from their mistakes and avoid the pain of the fall?

3. Even though it was his brother who made terrible choices, Tyler was feeling the pain of worry and sadness. What does that tell you about the effects of making poor choices?

Our Own Front Gate

Sasha was a young girl who lived just outside the city of Jerusalem more than two thousand years ago. One morning she came downstairs for breakfast, very excited. "Mother," she said, "I had the most wonderful dream last night. I dreamed that Jesus was going to pass by our house today on the way to Jerusalem. I imagine that if he comes, he will be riding in a chariot drawn by pure white horses!"

"Well," replied her mother, "He may come by but I'm not sure about the chariot." Sasha continued, "Travelers who have stopped at our well for water have told me that he heals the sick, helps the poor, and teaches everyone to love one another." Her mother

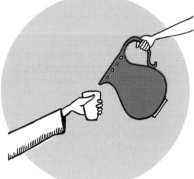

smiled and asked, "How could he help others if he rides by so fast?" After a soft kiss on the forehead, she told her daughter to go ahead and wait outside to see who might pass by that day.

"Thank you, Mother," replied Sasha eagerly. "I will stand by the fence all day and watch for him. I will even pack a lunch so that I won't have to come in to eat."

Daylight had barely begun, but Sasha didn't want to risk missing the one she heard so much about. She packed a lunch of lentils, flat bread, and dates and hurried out to watch for the one she had dreamed would pass.

The young girl watched by the gate all day long. As it grew dark, she came into the house smiling and seemed to be very happy. Sasha's mother placed her arms around her daughter and asked, "All day long you have been watching and waiting. Did Jesus pass by our house?"

"I'm not sure, Mother. There was an old man who came by and I gave him a drink from our well. I took a thorn from the paw of a dog; the poor thing was limping terribly. I lifted a small bird, that had fallen, back into its nest. I saw an old woman who appeared to be awfully hungry and so I shared my lunch with her."

Sasha's mother hugged her closely and warmly. "Yes, Sasha," she said, "I think Jesus did pass by our house today. He passed by in all the good things you did for others. You did the things that he, too, would have done. Today, you were the heart and hands of Jesus right at our own front gate."

CHAT BOX

1. Why do you think that Sasha imagined that Jesus might come by in a beautiful, horse-drawn chariot?

2. What did Sasha's mother mean by telling Sasha that she was "the heart and hands of Jesus" right at their own front gate?

3. Why do you think Sasha came in with a smile on her face even though she wasn't sure if Jesus had passed by?

The Stone in the Road

Once there was a king who was very upset with his townspeople. Everyone was in the habit of waiting for others to do the things that needed to be done.

One evening, the king went down to the narrow road leading into town. He dug a large hole in the middle of the road. He opened his royal cloak and pulled out a small velvet bundle and placed it into the hole. He then rolled a very large stone over it, jumped onto his white, regal horse, and trotted back to his castle.

The next morning a farmer, pulling his cart down the road, noticed the large stone. "This is terrible!" he said. "People are so lazy. Many have passed this road lately, but no one was kind enough to move this huge rock. People these days!" he snarled. He struggled to move his cart past the stone and continued down the road.

Next, a troop of soldiers came marching down the narrow way. Their leader, seeing the stone, halted the soldiers. He ordered them

HOT·NUTS·

to split up so that they could march around either side of the stone. After they passed, he made a speech about carelessness. "This stone," he shouted, "probably dropped off of someone's wagon, but he was too lazy to stop and remove it." With that, he commanded his soldiers to continue marching down the hillside. The stone was left where they had found it.

Later in the day, some peddlers with horses carrying exotic spices and herbs were traveling down the road. "This is some lousy country. They don't even take care of their roads!" said one of the

men. The other began grumbling. "I wonder how long that large stone has been there!" he said. Neither of them suggested moving the stone. Like the soldiers, the peddlers divided and passed to the right and left of it.

Day after day, people passed the stone in the middle of the road, blaming everyone else for not moving it. Finally, the king sent word to the townspeople to meet him at the stone.

"I put this large rock here," he said. "For three weeks, many of you have passed by and have blamed your neighbors for not removing it. None of you took it upon yourself to move it to the side of the road." The people could hear the disappointment in the king's voice.

The king walked over to the stone and began to move it. Some of his subjects offered to help, but he refused. The stone was not very heavy or difficult to lift. The king knelt down, reached into the hole in the ground, and pulled out the bundle wrapped in royal purple velvet. On the bag, was a note that read: "FOR WHOMEVER

REMOVES THE STONE." The king untied the string, turned the bag upside down, and out poured a stream of golden coins. The king's subjects were in shock. "Ah, if only I had taken the time to move the stone," someone said. Others were silent, feeling ashamed and disappointed that they had done nothing.

The townspeople learned a valuable lesson. They knew they probably wouldn't find a bag of gold coins under the rubbish they picked up from the ground, or by moving the next big rock in the middle of the road. They did realize, however, that rewards come from just knowing that they helped to make life easier for someone else and by helping to make this world a more beautiful place to live.

CHAT BOX

1. Why did the king place his own valuable gold coins into the hole?

2. Does it make sense that so many travelers complained about the stone yet did not move it? Why?

3. Why did the king refuse help moving the stone?

4. Do you help keep things beautiful without being asked?

Philip's House

Philip was a boy who was very clever with his hands. He loved to use tools and build things. He decided that when he grew up he would learn how to build houses.

After Philip graduated from college, he set up an office in town and waited for someone to hire him to build a house. Several weeks went by and no one had knocked. He began to worry whether he would ever have work to do. Finally he received a visit from Mr. Goulet, the

richest man in town. Philip's eyes opened wide. Could it be possible that the very wealthy Mr. Goulet wanted him to build a house?

"Philip," said Mr. Goulet, "I have watched you for a number of years and I have admired the way you have worked to get through college. I like seeing a young person who isn't afraid to work. This is why I came to you." He continued. "I am going overseas for about six months. While I am gone I want you to build a house for me. I own a vacant lot near your office that you can build on and I have $300,000 in the bank especially for you to use. Do the best you can with that budget. Keep a record of all your costs for me to see when I return." Mr. Goulet gave a quick wave and walked out of the door.

It seemed too good to be true. Philip grabbed his coat and hat and hurried off to tell his fiancé the news. After many days of planning, Philip was ready to start building. When he went to the cement company, he noticed two different types of cement. One bag of cement cost twice as much as the other. When he inquired as to the reason, the salesman told him that one was a better quality.

Philip began to think. "I could make a bigger profit if I bought the cheaper bags of cement and charged Mr. Goulet for the more expensive ones. He would never know. Besides, he has more money than he needs." So Philip used the cheaper cement to build the foundation of the house and made the records appear differently. He decided to do the same thing throughout the house, using cheaper materials yet charging the more expensive price. He used lower quality lumber, wiring, plumbing parts, and other necessary materials.

Finally the house was completed and it looked beautiful. However, it was not as good as it looked for it was built of poor materials.

When Mr. Goulet returned and went to look at the house, he complimented Philip on the wonderful job he had done. "I have never seen a finer house anywhere. You have done a masterful job. It is better than I had hoped. I told you how much I admired your spirit in completing school, and I also knew that you wanted to get married but couldn't afford it. Well, son," he paused, "my wife and I wanted to give you a nice wedding gift. This house is all yours!"

No one could be more flabbergasted and embarrassed. Mr. Goulet had treated him with much trust, kindness and respect. Yet Philip had repaid him dishonorably. Philip realized that he deserved nothing more than to be living in a house made with low-quality materials. After what he had done, he didn't feel that he deserved the house at all. Or did he?

CHAT BOX

1. If Philip had been completely truthful and had used the best materials to build the house, what kind of home could he have owned?

2. In the end, who did Philip cheat more, himself or Mr. Goulet?

3. Should Philip tell Mr. Goulet what he did?

4. Our lives are the "homes" we build. If everything we do or say adds something to our "house," how can we make it the very best? Give examples.

5. Would Philip feel better about accepting the generous gift if he told Mr. Goulet what he had done?

Acres of Diamonds

This is a true story about a farmer in Africa who was going about his daily routine when a visitor knocked at the door. The man was very excited about looking for diamonds. The excitement of the visitor was so contagious that the farmer decided that he, too, wanted to go in search of the precious gemstones.

The farmer immediately sold his farm and set out in hopes of striking it rich by discovering diamond mines. He wandered all over the African continent, scouting, digging and searching for diamonds. He never found a single one. After years of searching, the farmer became completely discouraged by the experience and felt despair and hopelessness. He finally sailed away and was never heard from again.

Meanwhile, back at the farm, the new owner was hard at work on his farming chores. One day he picked up an unusual looking rock on the property and placed it on the mantle of his fireplace. It was the size of a very large egg. A visitor came by the farm to speak with the new owner. When he stepped into the house, his eyes nearly popped out of his head. He saw the rock on the mantle and was stunned. The visitor told the new owner that the rock on his mantle was the biggest diamond he had ever seen. The new owner was struck in amazement. "Why my whole farm is covered with these things!" he exclaimed.

The new farm owner was absolutely correct. His farm was covered with diamonds! His property turned out to contain the richest diamond mine the world has ever known and the new owner quickly became one of the world's richest men.

Of course the old owner of the property had no idea that his farm was covered in diamonds. He was sure that riches must surely lie "somewhere out there." So he gave up his own way of life for the exciting promise of "striking it rich." Sadly, he never found any diamonds along the way. If he had only looked right in his own back yard, he would have found the wealth right under his nose.

CHAT BOX

1. Was it smart for the farmer to sell his land because one person caused excitement about the possibilities of striking it rich somewhere else?

2. What might have happened if the original owner had done his homework, studying about diamonds and diamond mines before he sold the farm?

3. Some people think that life would be better if they lived in a different family. Do you think there could be "diamonds" in your own family that you might be overlooking?

The Elephant and the Thrush

One day in the African jungle an elephant and a thrush became engaged in an argument as to whose voice could be heard the farthest. The elephant told the thrush that she was foolish to even raise the question. With an attitude just as showy as her feathers, she insisted that her voice could carry just as far or farther than the voice of the elephant. To settle the argument they decided to have a contest. All the animals of the forest would be called as judges.

Without letting the other animals know, the thrush called a secret meeting of the thrush clan. "Friends," she said, "I'm afraid I opened my mouth too soon. I told the elephant that my voice could penetrate the forest as far as his and farther. He challenged me to a contest. I'm in trouble and need your help." One of the birds didn't want to listen and said, "Lilly, you got yourself into this mess and we shouldn't have to bail you out!"

Another member of the thrush community spoke up and said, "The elephant is always bragging. It would be a great joke! Let's listen to her plan." Lilly continued to explain her idea. "We will station ourselves at hundred-yard intervals in the forest. When I stand next to the elephant and begin to sound my note, the next thrush in hiding will pick it up and sing. The note will carry to the next bird that will carry it and so on, and so on. In this way, we can send our song all the way through the forest.

After Lilly explained her plan, all the birds took a vote and agreed to play this trick on the elephant.

The day of the contest arrived and the elephant gave a bellow that nearly shook the leaves from all the trees. Then Lilly sounded one clear beautiful note from her tiny throat. The moment the sound of

 89

that note died down, another thrush one hundred yards away took up the note and carried it on, and then another and another.

The judges began moving through the forest. They asked the animals if they had heard the elephant. "Indeed we did. The sound shook the ground beneath our feet." "Did you hear the thrush?" they asked another. "Yes we did. Her note was clear and sweet and easily heard." The judges moved through the forest another hundred yards or so. "Did you hear the elephant?" they asked. "Yes we did," the animals answered. It was a mighty roar, but we heard the thrush, too. Her note was clear and beautiful."

And so it went. Checkpoint after checkpoint, the animal judges could hear both the elephant and the thrush. When they had continued two miles into the jungle, the questions were asked again. However, this time the answer was, "We could not hear the large elephant's trumpet, but we could hear the sweet gentle sound of the thrush."

The judges declared Lilly, the thrush, the winner. All the thrushes gathered together and chuckled over the joke they had played on the elephant. But, because the small birds had good souls, they eventually let the elephant in on their little secret - one small voice when linked to many others can carry a beautiful song for miles and miles.

CHAT BOX

1. Why should we be careful about what we tell other people?

2. What could Lilly, the thrush, have done differently so that she would not have had to involve her friends in a scheme to trick the elephant?

3. Was it right for the thrushes to play this trick on the elephant?

4. Are you glad that the thrushes eventually told the elephant what they had done? Why or why not?

Free To Be

There once was a colony of chimpanzees that lived deep in a jungle. They had a good life in the forest. They drank from the cool, fresh jungle streams, slept high in the trees and ate lots of fresh fruit.

One day, a very special baby chimp was born. His name was Scotty. Scotty was different. As he grew up, he began to hang out with the girl chimps and to help the mother chimps take care of the baby chimps. He loved to race through the trees, climbing up and down and over the branches and limbs with the little ones clinging to his back. The baby chimps laughed and hooted and loved playing with Scotty.

However, not everyone thought that it was a good idea for Scotty to help with the baby chimps. Some of the clan elders were not pleased. Many of the other boy chimps called him "sissy" and did not want to play with him.

The elder chimps held a council meeting. "It is not right for a young boy chimp to help raise the babies!" said Mr. Pat, one of the elders. "This is the type of job that only the mothers and the girl chimps should do!" "He does not belong in the nursery," argued a lady elder. "Something must be done!" shouted another. "This just isn't the way we usually do things around here," they all agreed.

After the meeting, the elders decided to forbid boy chimps from helping in the chimpanzee nursery. Poor Scotty! He was told that he could no longer play with the little chimps.

Day after day, Scotty became sadder and sadder. He did not race through the trees anymore. He did not laugh and play. Life seemed to drain out of him.

Finally, the mothers and auntie chimps had enough and demanded a meeting with the elders. "This is not right," they said. "We are all different. Scotty is a big help to us and he loves the work of caring for the little chimps. Helping in the nursery is a good thing, not a bad thing. It shouldn't matter if he is a boy! In this tribe, we should all be free to be what we want to be!"

Many of the elders realized that they had been wrong. The chief elder made a speech to the others. "The mother chimps are right," he said. "Youngsters and oldsters alike should be 'free to be.'" The chief elder realized that he, too, should be "free to be" someone who would make the right choices. He was not afraid if others disagreed, or if he lost his popularity. So the elders made a new rule that all chimpanzees were free to help the tribe in whatever way they desired.

Scotty, once again, was allowed to serve the tribe with his talents, whether or not others approved.   Most of the chimps thought that being "free to be" was such a good idea that they made up a song and a dance. They decided to have a party to celebrate. There was singing and swinging until the early morning hours.   What a celebration that was!

CHAT BOX

1. Who do you know who is different, like Scotty the chimp? Is it okay for this person to be different?

2. What do you think is meant by the sentence, "the life seemed to drain out of him"?

3. Do you think that someone is genuinely free if he or she only makes decisions based on what others think?

4. Should you be free to be hurtful to others?

Dr. DALE TURNER attended West Virginia Wesleyan College because of its athletic program – he had intended to become a high school football coach. Upon graduating, he changed directions and accepted a scholarship to Yale Divinity School. DR. Turner began his career as a minister in Michigan in 1943. He spent 10 years in Lawrence, Kansas, teaching at the University of Kansas and preaching at the Plymouth Congregational Church. He moved to Seattle in 1958 to lead the University Congregational Church. He retired in 1982 and began writing a weekly column for the Religion page of the Seattle Times, which he still writes today. He has become one of the most widely read Religion Page columnists in the country.

Dr. Turner helped pay his way through college and divinity school by working as a magician for children's events. This skill served him well as a pastor, using it as part of his work with children. A regular feature of his Sunday morning service was the "sermonette." Given primarily for the children, it was enjoyed by all. Filled with magic, live animals, and other theatrics, the sermonettes amused and provided a valuable life lesson.

Dr. Turner lives in Seattle with his wife of 53 years, Leone. They have four sons, three daughters-in-law, six grandsons, and two granddaughters. Dr. Turner can be reached at www.askdrt.org.

ROSS T. SMART grew up on a small farm in Sanbornton, New Hampshire. His life journey has taken him to places as diverse as Tanzania and Alaska. Currently he makes his home in Seattle, Washington.

According to his mother, Ross began work as an artist at the age of three when he broke his leg. Having little to do, he whiled away the time by creating sculptures out of window putty. His career took a major step forward when he attended Plymouth State College for Fine Arts in New Hampshire. His paintings and drawings have been displayed in Skagway, Alaska and in Seattle, Washington. Most recently a collection of paintings based on his Tanzanian experience were displayed at Monkey Business, a popular Seattle art gallery.

Free to Be is Ross' first illustration of a children's book and his wonderful, whimsical style adds a special touch to these timeless teaching stories. Ross can be reached at www.rosstsmart.com.